EDGE
BOOKS™

DRAWING COOL STUFF

HOW TO DRAW

INCREDIBLE
CARS

by Aaron Sautter
illustrated by Brian Bascle

Capstone
press®
Mankato, Minnesota

Edge Books are published by Capstone Press,
1710 Roe Crest Drive, North Mankato, Minnesota 56003.
www.capstonepub.com

Books published by Capstone Press are manufactured with paper
containing at least 10 percent post-consumer waste.

Library of Congress Cataloging-in-Publication Data
Sautter, Aaron.
    How to draw incredible cars / by Aaron Sautter; illustrated by Brian Bascle.
    p. cm.—(Edge books. Drawing cool stuff)
    Includes bibliographical references and index.
    Summary: "Lively text and fun illustrations describe how to draw
incredible cars"—Provided by publisher.
    ISBN–13: 978-1-4296-0077-4 (hardcover)
    ISBN–10: 1-4296-0077-2 (hardcover)
    1. Automobiles in art—Juvenile literature. 2. Drawing—Technique—Juvenile
literature. I. Bascle, Brian. II. Title. III. Series.
NC825.A8S28 2008
743'.89629222—dc22   2007003453

Credits
Jason Knudson, designer

Printed in the United States of America in North Mankato, Minnesota.
022012   006616R

TABLE OF CONTENTS

WELCOME!

You probably picked this book because you love really cool cars. Or maybe you picked it because you like to draw. Whatever the reason, get ready to dive into the world of incredible cars!

People have been traveling in cars for more than a hundred years. During that time, cars have come in many shapes and sizes. From the Model-T Fords of the early 1900s to the futuristic cars of tomorrow, people love driving their cars wherever they go.

This book is just a starting point. Once you've learned to draw the cool cars in this book, you can start drawing your own. Let your imagination run wild, and see what kinds of incredible cars you can create!

To get started, you'll need some supplies:

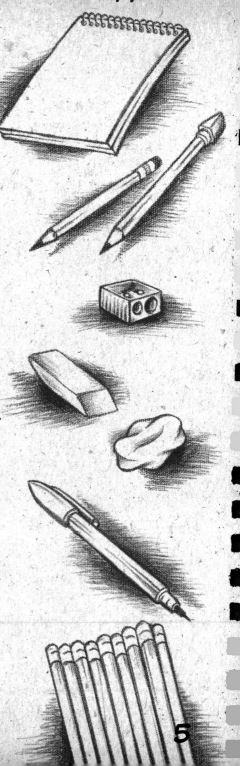

1. First you'll need drawing paper. Any type of blank, unlined paper will do.

2. Pencils are the easiest to use for your drawing projects. Make sure you have plenty of them.

3. You have to keep your pencils sharp to make clean lines. Keep a pencil sharpener close by. You'll use it a lot.

4. As you practice drawing, you'll need a good eraser. Pencil erasers wear out very fast. Get a rubber or kneaded eraser. You'll be glad you did.

5. When your drawing is finished, you can trace over it with a black ink pen or thin felt-tip marker. The dark lines will really make your work stand out.

6. If you decide to color your drawings, colored pencils and markers usually work best. You can also use colored pencils to shade your drawings and make them more lifelike.

1950s Classic: Front View

The 1950s are often called the "Golden Age of Cars." Specially shaped lights, white-wall tires, chrome grills, and other details made the cars unique. Sometimes special hood ornaments really helped set a car apart from the rest.

After drawing this car, try it again using your own unique designs.

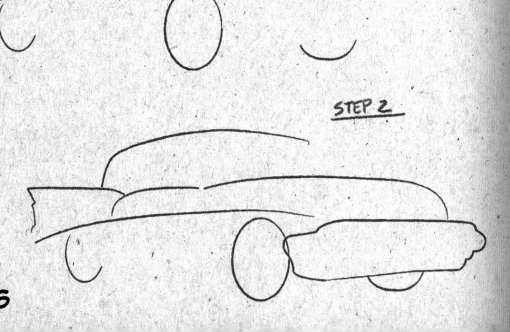

STEP 1

STEP 2

STEP 3

STEP 4

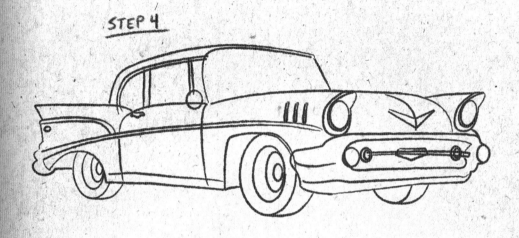

FINAL!

7

1950s CLASSIC: REAR VIEW

Cars from the 1950s had special features from hood to trunk. Tail fins often stood high on the back end. Colorful paint jobs and other features gave each car loads of personality!

Keep trying out new designs. How big can you make the tail fins on this car?

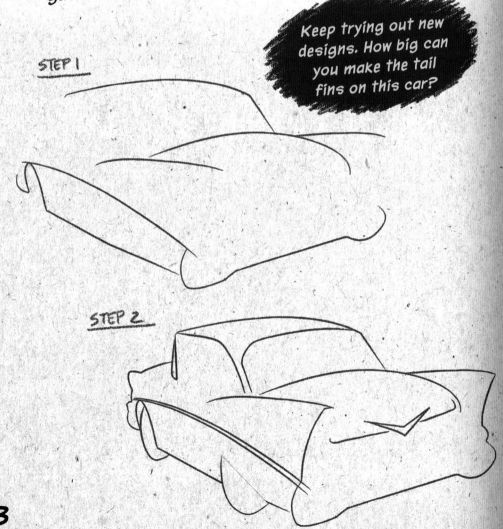

STEP 1

STEP 2

STEP 3

STEP 4

FINAL!

1957

9

ROADSTER FUN

Sports cars of the 1950s had a sleek, streamlined look. They rode close to the ground and had curvy shapes to gain an extra bit of speed. These sporty roadsters let drivers fly down the road in style.

After you've finished drawing this car, try it again with the top down. Nothing beats a ride in a sporty convertible!

STEP 1

STEP 2

STEP 4

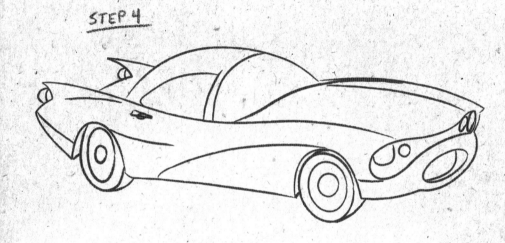

FINAL!

11

RAYZR-XT

People have always dreamed of what cars would look like in the future. We can only imagine the features cars might have 50 years from now. The RAYZR-XT is only one possible design for the car of the future.

After practicing this drawing, try creating your own futuristic car. What kind of car can you imagine?

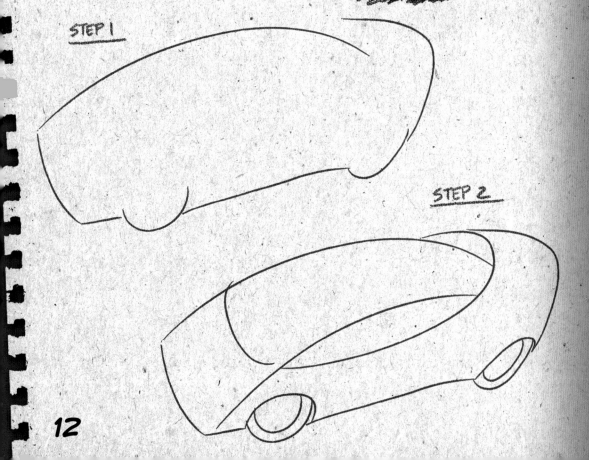

STEP 1

STEP 2

STEP 3

STEP 4

FINAL!

13

PHANTOM

Many early cars were built with style in mind. Luxury cruisers like the Phantom often had curvy fenders and hoods. Driving one of these cars showed you had fine taste in automobiles. Be careful not to scratch the paint!

After drawing this car, try giving it a stylish hood ornament shaped like your favorite fast animal.

STEP 1

STEP 2

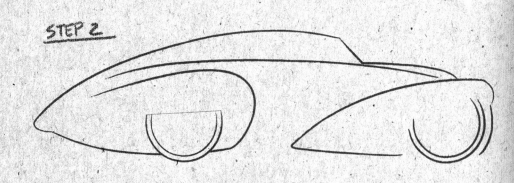

STEP 3

STEP 4

FINAL!

DELTA GLIDER

The Delta Glider can't really fly, but it feels like it could take flight at any time. This sporty concept roadster features gull-wing doors with a futuristic look. This sleek beauty can really cruise down the road. Just don't bump your head when you get out!

After drawing this car, try giving it some cool new features of your own.

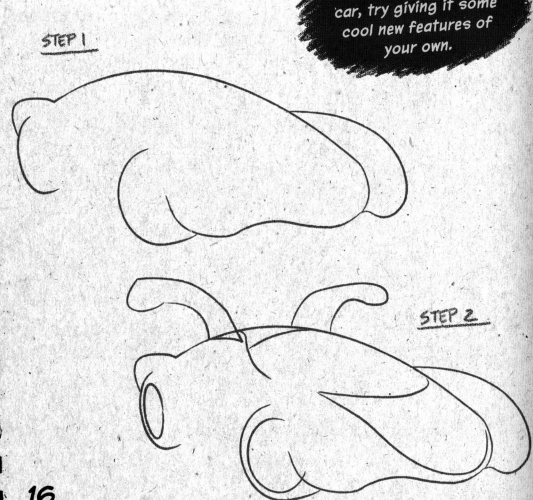

STEP 1

STEP 2

STEP 3

STEP 4

FINAL!

17

HOT ROD XTREME

Lots of people like to turn old cars into hot rods. They add large tires and snazzy body parts to make their cars stand out. Sometimes they paint flames on the side or add lots of chrome to create a unique look.

When you're done drawing this hot rod, try adding some flames on the side for a cool street racer look!

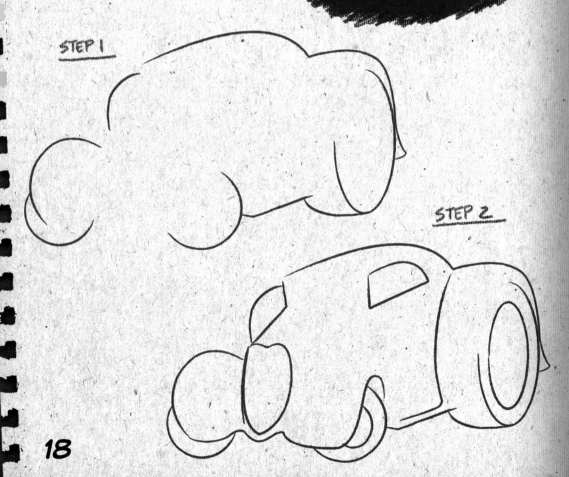

STEP 1

STEP 2

STEP 3

STEP 4

FINAL!

19

POWER DRAG

Awesome power and incredible speed often come to mind when talking about dragsters. These explosive machines can top speeds of 300 miles per hour. No wonder they need parachutes to help them stop at the end of a race!

After drawing this car, try adding a second one to compete with it on the track.

STEP 1

STEP 2

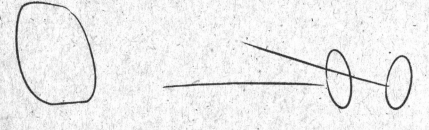

STEP 3

STEP 4

FINAL!

HOPPER

Some people like driving and customizing lowriders. Sometimes they add hydraulic systems to create a hopping lowrider. These cars often have one, two, or all four tires set up to bounce or hop the car into the air.

When you're done with this drawing, try it again with even more tires bouncing the car into the air!

STEP 1.

STEP 2.

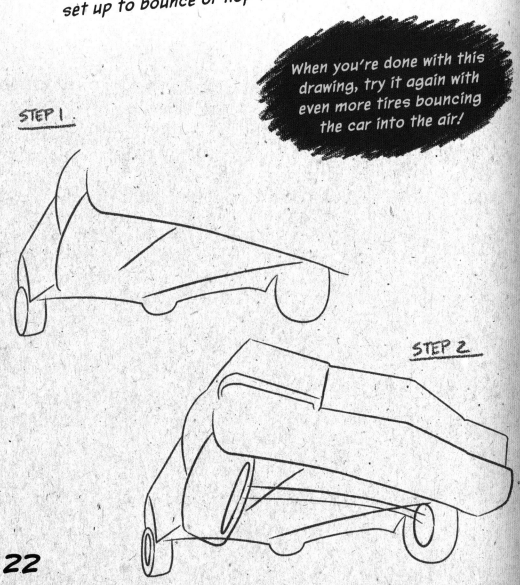

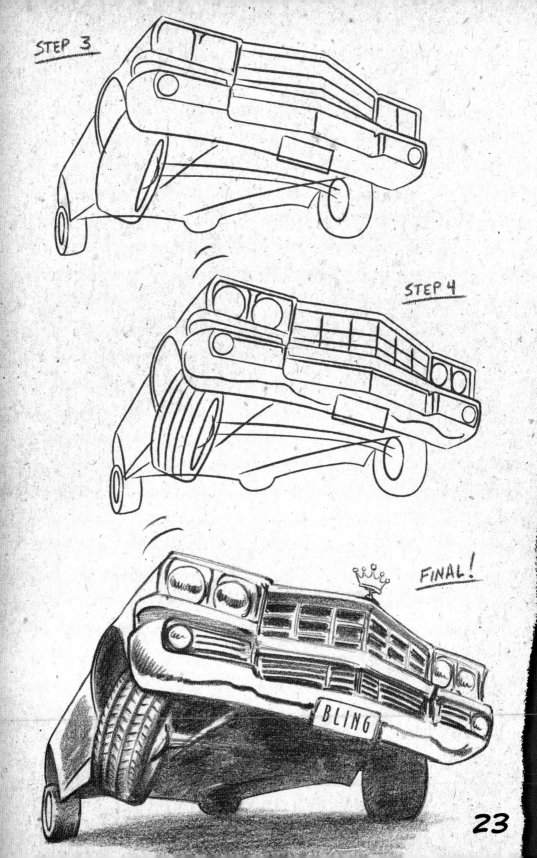

STEP 3

STEP 4

FINAL!

BLING

1960s MUSCLE

The 1960s saw the rise of the muscle car. Many muscle cars were sporty convertibles. Nothing quite compares with putting the top down and letting the wind blow through your hair. Let's go for a drive!

When you're done with this car, try drawing yourself and a friend taking it for a spin around town!

STEP 1

STEP 2

STEP 3

STEP 4

FINAL!

AT THE RACES

The danger! The wrecks! The photo finishes! Stock car racing thrills fans at every turn. Huge engines power stock cars up to 200 miles per hour. Cover your ears as they go by—the roar of the engines can be deafening!

When you've mastered this drawing, try creating some stock cars of your own. Which do you think could win in a race?

STEP 1

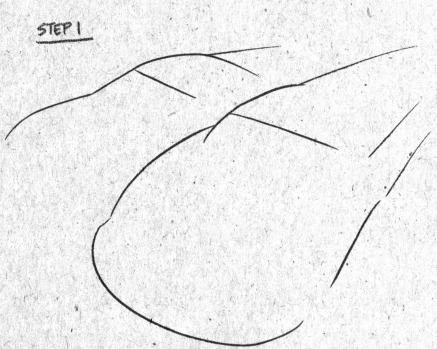

STEP 2

STEP 3

TO FINISH THIS DRAWING,
TURN TO THE <u>NEXT PAGE</u>!

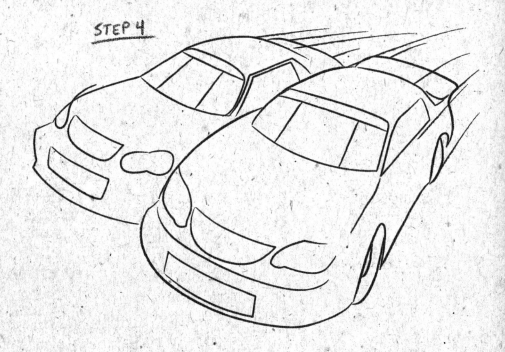

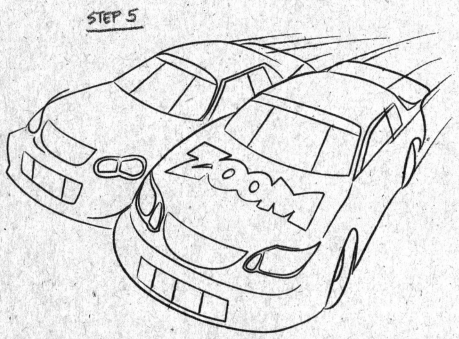

STEP 6

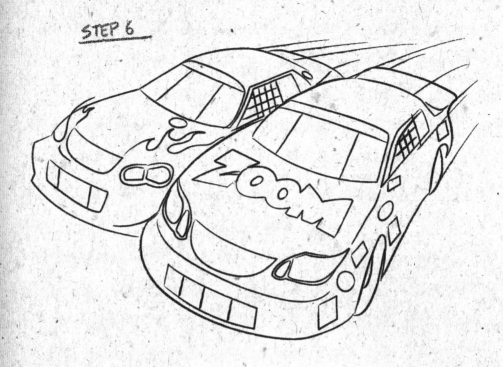

FINAL!

GLOSSARY

concept (KON-sept)—an idea for a new way to build or create something

convertible (kuhn-VUR-tuh-buhl)—a car with a top that can be put down

customize (KUHSS-tuh-mize)—to change a vehicle according to the owner's needs and tastes

hydraulic system (hye-DRAW-lik SISS-tuhm)—a system of pumps powered by fluid forced through chambers or pipes to raise and lower a car

ornament (OR-nuh-muhnt)—a small object used as a decoration

parachute (PAIR-uh-shoot)—a large piece of strong fabric that flies out behind a dragster at the end of a race to help slow down the car

streamlined (STREEM-lined)—designed to move easily and quickly through the air

unique (yoo-NEEK)—one of a kind

READ MORE

Barr, Steve. *1-2-3 Draw Cartoon Cars: A Step by Step Guide.* 1-2-3 Draw. Columbus, N.C.: Peel Productions, 2005.

Court, Rob. *How to Draw Cars and Trucks.* Doodle Books. Chanhassen, Minn.: Child's World, 2007.

Harpster, Steve. *Cars and Trucks.* Pencil, Paper, Draw! New York: Sterling, 2006.

INTERNET SITES

FactHound offers a safe, fun way to find Internet sites related to this book. All of the sites on FactHound have been researched by our staff.

Here's how:
1. Visit *www.facthound.com*
2. Choose your grade level.
3. Type in this book ID code **1429600772** for age-appropriate sites. You may also browse subjects by clicking on letters, or by clicking on pictures and words.
4. Click on the **Fetch It** button.

FactHound will fetch the best sites for you!

INDEX